HOW NOT TO GET SHOT BY COPS

A SURVIVAL GUIDE TO POLICE ENCOUNTERS

BY: JOHN W. BRYSON III

Copyright © 2016 All Right Reserved.

ISBN: 978-0-578-18945-1

TABLE OF CONTENTS

INTRODUCTION

If the police have ever shot you, then my best guess is that you've come here because you want to learn all of the best ways to prevent it from ever happening again. I can imagine what's going through your head right now, probably "I'm lucky to be alive but if it happened once, then it can happen again." As the author of "How Not To Get Shot By The Cops" I would like to say that even though I haven't been shot by a police officer, I still feel your pain.

I was raised in Carol City, FL now Called Miami Gardens; FL in the 1980's and 1990's at the heels of the "Cocaine Cowboy" era. The stories, and song lyrics of famous rapper Rick Ross *(who also boasts being raised in Carol City)* was, and is an everyday reality for many. Currently, the city of Miami Gardens has a homicide rate higher than New York and Chicago. In 2014 Miami Gardens earned the title of the "Stop-and-Frisk Capital of America" following a Fusion Network investigation that revealed police officers had stopped and questioned 56,992 people – more than half of the city's population -- between 2008 and 2013. Out of those 56,992 people stopped, none of them were arrested; they were regular law-abiding citizens. Living in a city for almost 30 years where almost everyone is considered a suspect, gave me the unwanted but useful experience of encountering the police via foot stops, car stops, consensual stops, curfew stops etc. Though these unwanted encounters were frustrating and most of the time unjust, I fortunately was never shot by law enforcement, which I attribute to the information and steps found in this book.

So why do some people get shot by the police while others like myself don't? For one, there's the matter of chance. Some things just go wrong in a police encounter and whether or not you deserve to be shot by the police, we are all at risk. But it's not just a matter of chance. According to data collected by the Washington Post, 990 people were shot dead by police in 2015. Out of all 990 people, 948 were males and 782 were carrying a deadly weapon. Now these numbers are no means the final tally. In 2015 the director of the FBI James Comey testified, " We can't have an informed discussion because we don't have data. People have data on who went to a movie last weekend or how many books were sold or how many cases of the flu walked into the emergency room and I cant tell you how many people were shot by police officers in the United States last month, last year or anything about the demographics". The numbers previously mentioned are most likely higher (*maybe even double or triple*) because it doesn't make sense for police departments to over report police shootings.

It probably comes as no surprise that carrying a deadly weapon makes it more likely to get shot by the police. On the other hand, you might be wondering why your gender or race, for example, makes you more likely to get shot by the police. Well, the answer is not so straightforward which is why I decided to write this book and explain everything you need to know about the problem at hand.

So if you are here to try and make sense of these anomalies or to figure out how you can reduce your chances of being shot by the police, then you are off to a good start, because by the time you finish reading this entire book I promise, you will have several solutions to both.

Recent Events

There is no certain date as to when all of the controversy surrounding police shootings in America started, but we do know that thousands of Americans are rallying behind social justice movements to voice their opinions on the matter.

The earliest and, perhaps, most controversial demonstrations are the Movement for Black Lives. The first Movement for Black Lives took place in Washington at the entrance of the Office of Police Complaints. Protesters held signs up with the words "Black Lives Matter" and "Stop Killing Black People."

The Stop Police Terror Project and Freedom Now are two other activist movements that have garnered national attention in recent months.

In July 2016, a police officer shot an unarmed therapist on the streets of North Miami, Florida. In a video that showed the events leading up to the shooting, the African American therapist Charles Kinsey is seen laying on the ground while holding his hands up in the air. Next to him is another man sitting upright. Not until after the shooting was it discovered that Kinsey was trying to help an autistic patient who had run away from his assisted living facility.

The police shooting of Charles Kinsey is just one example of several recent police shootings of African American males that have sparked major public outrage across the nation. The deaths of African American men by police officers in particular is now a nationwide problem. Police shootings also took place in Staten Island, NY; Cleveland, OH; Baltimore, MD; Ferguson, MO; and North Charleston, S.C., to name a few.

However, it should also be mentioned that recent attacks on police officers have also contributed to an increasingly violent environment. Recently, a heavily armed sniper opened fire on police officers in Dallas, Texas. The shooter took five police officer lives after two African American men in Minnesota and Louisiana were recently shot and killed by white police officers.

The fact that we are seeing an increasing amount of law abiding citizens shot by police officers suggests that no one is entirely exempt from police shootings. It's more important than ever to be prepared for all police encounters. The recent events that have swarmed our smart phones, televisions, and newspapers encourage us to ask ourselves how we can keep ourselves and our families safe from acts of violence. While the police-citizen situation is surrounded by an overwhelming amount of controversy and debate, one thing is certain: We must have the shared goal of moving forward and participating in effective solutions to the problem—no matter what opinion we may have on recent events.

You Should Read This Book If:

- You were shot by the police and survived and you never want it to happen again.
- The police haven't shot you, but you want to prepare for anything and everything.
- You came close to getting shot by the police
- You live in America.
- You live in a Stop and Frisk prone city.
- You carry a weapon for self-defense.
- You're a male.
- You walk a lot.
- You get suspicious looks from police officers.
- You're an African-American male.
- You drive a lot.
- You have a tendency to freak out in stressful situations.
- You want to know about police shootings and why issues of race, gender, and class matter.
- You have seen the news in the past six months.
- You don't fall into any of these categories but you love your life and would rather not die during a police encounter.

Chapter 1. Move To Another Country

If you have watched the news in the last six or so months, then there is no doubt you've heard about all of the recent police shootings in the United States. Thousands of upset American citizens are retaliating and questioning police across the country on their ability to protect the communities they serve.

Many protestors and critics bring up the fact that in other countries citizens aren't getting shot by the police. It's true too. Last year, The Guardian compared the amount of police shootings in the US and England & Wales. In the United States, there were 59 fatal police shootings in the <ins>first 24 days of 2015</ins>. On the other hand, there were 55 fatal police shootings in England & Wales in the <ins>last 24 years.</ins>

If moving to another country is not an option for you, then that's okay because there will be plenty of other ways to not get shot by the police in the rest of this book. But if you want to statistically reduce your chances of being shot by the police; moving to lets say England or Wales is an option.

Moving To Another Country

You may have heard that police shootings are more common in the U.S than in other nations around the world. It's true too—America is one of the only world leaders with a large volume of police shootings. Why? Well, there is no clear or definitive explanation, but we do know some things that may clear the situation up a little bit.

Our gun laws may explain the biggest difference between the U.S. and our European counterparts. As you may know, the Second Amendment protects our right "to bear arms." Our purpose is to not bash gun ownership or gun rights, but, rather, to try and make sense of the situation in which innocent Americans are dying at the hands of police officers. Gun ownership may contribute to a higher amount of police shootings because it means that our police officers are trained to take extra precautions during civilian encounters to reduce the risk of being shot.

To touch on this last note, another possible reason for the frequency of police shootings in the U.S. compared to other nations is police training. A police officer's job is by no means easy nor straightforward. Decisions are made within a matter of seconds during the highly stressful situations they deal with on a daily basis. Much of their training involves videos of police officers being shot down, disarmed, or badly beaten just a few moments upon arriving to a scene. As a result, the police are trained to avoid hesitation and make a quick judgment about a particular threat level.

We will cover some of the ways that police officers could improve their training throughout the rest of this book, but for now an understanding of police training tactics can explain why we must take police encounters very seriously to avoid an escalated encounter.

If you have ever been out of the country before, then you should know something about other democratic nations. For one, the majority of them do not share our affinity for guns. Most of them typically have few violent confrontations in comparison to America.

The following police encounters may raise some eyebrows about American police force training and handling of aggressive situations. In the UK, last year, a man wielding a large machete threatened to kill several police officers right outside Buckingham Palace in London. The London police asked the man to lower his weapon, kept their distance and shot him with a Taser. Soon after, the situation was resolved as the man fell to the ground, temporarily incapacitated as the police officers proceeded to detain him.

A similar situation in St. Louis had a much different ending. In 2014 Kajieme Powell, a 25-year-old African American man, was recorded wielding a knife and walking towards several police officers who repeatedly told him to drop the weapon. When Powell didn't drop the weapon, the officers fired their weapons at him. The police shot Powell nine times at close range. When questioned by the media, the St. Louis Police Chief, Sam Dotson defended the officers' use of lethal force, claiming Tasers to be inadequate to resolve lethal situations.

Dotson said, "Certainly a Taser is an option that's available to the officers. But Tasers aren't 100 percent. So you've got an individual with a knife who's moving towards you, not listening to any verbal commands, He continues walking and says, 'shoot me now, kill me now'. Tasers aren't 100 percent. If that Taser misses, that [individual] continues on and hurts an officer."

While these are only two instances of the differences between police encounters in the U.S. and in the U.K., they represent a larger phenomenon, which has yet to be intensely studied to determine any conclusive evidence as to why police shootings are more common in the U.S. than in other countries. That being said, our first option to not get shot by the police is to move out of the country.

Regardless of how realistic or unrealistic moving out of the country may seem to you, it can be done. Of course, it takes dedication and commitment to make it happen. For some, moving to another country will be much easier than for the general population. Money gets you places but we're going to talk about several ways you may be able to move to another country.

1. Countries with the lowest rates of police shootings

America is an outlier in terms of police shootings. According to data from the Guardian, England & Wales had a total of 55 fatal police shootings in the last 24 years as of 2015. On the other hand, fatal police shootings reached a total of 59 within the first 24 days of the 2015 in the U.S. In the past 71 years of Iceland's existence, there has only been 1 fatal police shooting. From 2010 to 2011, there were 15 citizens of any race, armed or unarmed, fatally shot in Germany. In contrast, there were 19 unarmed African American men fatally shot by police in the first five months of 2015. In Australia, there were 94 fatal police shootings between 1992 and 2011. In the United States, there were 97 fatal police shootings in March 2015 alone. In Finland, where police serve over 5 million people, police fired only 6 bullets in 2013. On the other hand, police shot a total of 17 bullets in the death of Antonio Zambrano-Montes in Pasco, WA, a city with a population of 67,599 people.

The data puts forth a good argument for moving to another country. At the same time, there are several legal and personal roadblocks that may prevent you from making the move to the UK, for example. The personal roadblocks are quite obvious, because, when it comes down to it, leaving America is not the most practical solution to the problem of police shootings. For many people, learning a new language is no easy task nor is leaving your family and friends behind as well as the home in which you were raised.

However, if you are serious about not getting shot by the police—or you just want to try out life in a new country—pay close attention to some of the things you would need to do to move to the UK.

The first thing you will need to do if you want to move to the UK, is to check their visa requirements. You can find this information on their government website, but here are some basic guidelines to get you through the process.

- Almost all immigrants will need a visa.
- A visa allows you to live and work in the UK.
- Pick the visa that is most relevant to your personal situation.
- Then go to visa4uk.fco.gov.uk to start your application process.

Secondly, you will need to learn the rights of British citizens. As the situation remains today, citizens have the right to live and work in the United Kingdom as well as countries in the European Union. This could change soon, given the recent Brexit referendum in June 2016. In the Brexit referendum, 51.8% of British citizens voted in favor of exiting the European Union, which would effectively dismantle their European Union rights.

There are several other ways to live in the UK if you find that applying for a visa is not the best option for you. For example, you can apply for a job in the UK. Your visa will last for the duration of the job and depend on the job type. Tier 2 visas are for high-demand industries. If you think you are eligible for this type of work because you already work for a multinational company, then you might be eligible to transfer to the UK. Tier 2 visas typically allot around three to six years of residency. Tier 5 visas are considered temporary work permits and they last for around six months to two years. A Tier 5 visa is good for individuals who do not work in a high-demand sector, but have a desire to work for a charity or a church as well as an athlete or entertainer. Lastly, you can apply for a Tier 1 visa which is designed for entrepreneurs looking to start a business in the UK. You have to make a multimillion-pound investment or be a recognized leader in your field to prove you're serious about it.

Maybe you don't actually want to work or you're just not ready to get into a steady career yet. In that case, you will want to consider applying for a UK educational institution. To do this, you will need a sufficient amount of money to support yourself and be able to speak the English language.

There are several other visas as well. You can apply for special circumstances such as family. In this case, you would be eligible on the basis of a relationship to your spouse, fiancé, partner of two or more years, or child. You can also apply for a visa if you have UK ancestry. To apply for this visa, you must have a grandparent born in the UK. Tier 5 Youth Mobility pertains to citizens of certain countries (like the United States) between the ages of 18 and 30. Lastly, there is the Visitor visa, which is probably the very last option you want to pursue. You can arrive on a visitor visa and then try to support yourself until you can land a job and apply for a worker permit. The visitor visa-worker permit route is not recommended, because your chances for approval are very slim.

Maybe you want to check the UK out before settling in completely. London has tons of hostels and relatively inexpensive hotels to stay at during your visit. If you think any of these options are viable ways to get out of the United States and into a country with very few instances of police shootings, then do your research, budget, and plan. Even if it seems unlikely that you'll be approved to live in the UK, there are several other countries that you can apply for as well.

CHAPTER 2. HAVE THE *COMPLEXION* FOR THE *PROTECTION*

Earlier we discussed the race factor in police shootings. Of all the **unarmed** men shot by police in 2015, 40% were African American. When black men make up only about 6% of the population, this means that they are disproportionately victimized in fatal police shootings. Out of the African American men shot by police officers, 25% suffered from a mental illness or were experiencing an emotional crisis.

The Guardian also found that young African American men were nine times more likely to be shot by police officers. In the survey, 60% of African American men reported feeling unfairly targeted and mistreated by police officers. One Miami Gardens native, Earl Sampson has been detained more than 200 times and arrested for trespassing at the place he works. Also, other studies show an explicit trend of giving more severe punishments to black men than their white counterparts.

The race factor remains as one of the major issues in police shootings. Our goal is to describe the situation in the most accurate manner possible and to endorse no particular political opinion on the matter. It is more important than ever to be aware of who may be at more risk and who should take the appropriate precautionary measures against police shootings.

Shootings Of Unarmed African Americans

The Washington Post's data on national police shootings reveals that police shot and killed 93 unarmed people in 2015. Out of these 93 people, 32 were White and 38 were African American; 90 were male and 3 were female. 44 of them were between the ages of 18 and 29; and 35 of them were between the ages of 30 and 44. Only 34 of these cases were reported as an attack in progress. Again, these numbers are most likely higher (*maybe even double or triple*) because according to the director of the FBI James Comey, the FBI doesn't have police shooting data.

So what's the story behind all of these police shootings? The answer is not a simple one. Otherwise, there would be no need for this book. The best way to understand how to not get shot by the police, is to understand the specific circumstances surrounding police shootings of unarmed individuals. By the end of it, we hope you will be more informed and, thus, better prepared to avoid getting shot by the police.

Bettie Jones, 55, was accidentally shot by police officers after answering a shared front door at her apartment in Chicago on December 26th, 2015. The police were responding to a domestic disturbance after a relative called the police department on Quintonio LeGrier, 19. The report indicated LeGrier was carrying a metal baseball bat on the second floor of his father's apartment where Jones also lived. LeGrier was suffering from mental health problems at the time. Prior to the police's arrival to the scene, Jones received a phone call from LeGrier's father who asked her to let the police officers in. Jones' boyfriend was present at the time of the shooting. According to him, LeGrier ran to the bottom of the staircase with his bat at the same time Ms. Jones opened the door for the arriving police. The unnamed boyfriend said, "Then the shooting just started coming – bam, bam, bam!" The tragedy struck a chord with the local community who remember Ms. Jones as a mother figure for several community members including her own children. The unfortunate event led many to ask if police receive adequate training on violent confrontations. Critics mention that stun guns could be used instead of deadly weapons which can lead to accidental deaths of unarmed persons.

Samuel DuBose, 43, was an unarmed African American man shot on July 19th, 2015 in Mt. Auburn, Ohio after a University of Cincinnati police officer attempted to stop him for a missing license plate. The police officer shot DuBose in the head after he tried to drive away. You can watch the body cam footage on our YouTube channel. His friends and family say DuBose was a talented music producer.

On June 15th, 2015 police officers shot an unarmed 22-year-old African American man, Kris Jackson, as he was trying to climb through a motel room window in South Lake Tahoe, California. The police arrived at the scene after receiving a report about a woman screaming. Jackon's girlfriend claimed the officers did not attempt to command him to stop prior to shooting. The officer was placed on paid administrative leave until the investigation ended.

Up to this point, the police shootings of unarmed African American people have contributed to the controversy surrounding the use of deadly weapons in police encounters. Many believe that a Taser should be used instead of a gun in stressful, uncertain situations. Eric Harris, an unarmed 44-year-old African American man, was shot in the back on April 2nd, 2015 in Tulsa, Oklahoma as other officers subdued Harris on the ground. You can watch the body cam footage on our YouTube channel. The shooting officer, Robert Bates, was a reserve deputy. He claimed to have accidentally discharged his gun instead of his Taser. In the video, a gunshot is heard followed by Bates saying, "Oh, I shot him. I'm sorry." The mistake cost Harris's life and resulted in Bates being charged with second-degree manslaughter. The shooting sparked a public debate about the city's criteria for reserve police officers. Bates, an insurance agent, was in his 70s. The Tulsa sheriff's department reportedly uses around 100 volunteer reserve officers like Bates. Eric Harris's family has since filed a lawsuit and are awaiting judgment.

Many police shootings involve mentally ill subjects. One such example is the death of Lavall Hall. The unarmed African American man, 25, was shocked with a stun gun and shot on February 15th, 2015 in Miami Gardens, Florida. Hall's mother called 911 after her son became violent and went outside in his underwear. The police arrived at the scene and Hall struck two police officers with the metal end of a broomstick. Upon being struck by the stun gun, Hall refused to drop the broomstick handle and was then shot five times by police after he charged at an officer. According to his family, Hall was diagnosed with a mood disorder and schizophrenia. You can watch the body cam footage on our YouTube channel

It might seem obvious to some but if you are a minority in America, then you will want to stay as far away from crime as possible. Keeping yourself in a safe living environment with positive role models is one of the best ways to reduce your chances of being shot by the police. Staying away from trouble is common sense to say the least, but it happens. Before you know it, you can end up in a dangerous encounter with the police and they might even mistake you for one of your friends. Don't take the risk of falling into someone else's problems. You owe it to yourself and your loved ones. No one wants to see you getting shot by the police and associating with the wrong type of people is like a fast-track to an unfortunate fate.

If you happen to be at the wrong place at the wrong time, then leave as soon as possible. Don't stick around to see what happens. Remove yourself from the line of danger. Being accidentally shot by the police is a common error made in perceivably dangerous situations. If the police question you then remain calm and follow their orders. You never want to raise your voice or become angry even if you know you had nothing to do with something.

While we realize it is easier said than done, the bottom line is to never get involved in a risky or dangerous situation if you do not have to.

The more you know the better off you are in a police stop. Pay close attention to the following sections because they will pertain to you regardless of your gender, "race," or age.

CHAPTER 3. HOME ENCOUNTERS

Your home is a place of safety. Most of us are fortunate to have a home and we know it as our place to recharge. Whether it's singing in the shower or dancing around the kitchen in undergarments, the home is often one of the few places we can truly be ourselves. That being said, there might not be anything worse than getting shot by the police in your own home. You might not think the police will be coming to your home any time soon. If so, then you are probably a very fortunate individual. But for many Americans, a home encounter with the police is not uncommon. Regardless of how often you may have encountered the police in your home, all Americans should be aware of how to handle such a situation.

Home Encounters

There are several circumstances in which you may find the police at your home. Things can escalate very quickly too. The police have no idea what or who might be inside and will be especially quick to react to any potential threat by something in or outside of your home. Police may be more likely to perceive you and your behaviors as potential threats. On the other hand, having someone else of authority in your home can trigger stressful or nervous reactions, which police may also perceive as reasonable cause for suspicion.

Recently, a man was accidentally shot and killed by the police when they showed up at the wrong house in Stockbridge, Georgia. The Caucasian Air Force Veteran , William Powell, 63, was shot in the neck by a police officer and died shortly after. The police officers were responding to a 911 call reporting gunshots and a woman yelling for help. Powell was carrying a handgun when the police showed up at his home and refused to put it down after being ordered to do so. According to Powell's mother, the man was leaving the garage with his handgun to investigate a potential intruder after his dogs began barking.

Several critics of the situation expressed the need for police to be more open about identifying themselves. It was later discovered that the 911 operator was not given an exact address.

"I think the police should identify themselves more if they show up at someone's house in the middle of the night, instead of just shining lights in their windows," "He's a fine man" said Darrell Cooper, who has known Powell for at least 30 years.

Communication errors between the dispatcher and the police are entirely out of your control. The situation teaches us several things about home encounters with the police. Most importantly, it can happen to anyone. Powell was a military veteran with three grown children. The neighborhood he lived in is often thought of as a safe area with many older residents. The big lesson? Everyone must be aware of how to handle a home encounter with the police. William Powell's death is just one example of how a home encounter can quickly escalate into much worse situations. Another tragic home encounter involved an elderly woman who was shot in her home by undercover police officers.

One elderly African American woman, Kathryn Johnston was 92 when three undercover officers entered her home in Northwest Atlanta on November 21, 2006. Johnston had lived in her home for 17 years. After cutting the metal burglar bars on Johnston's door. The three officers broke down her door with a no-knock warrant.

{ A no-knock warrant is issued by a judge and it permits police to enter a home without notifying the residents immediately before (e.g. ringing a doorbell or knocking). The purpose of a no-knock warrant is to find suspected evidence before it can be destroyed. }

The police claimed that Johnston fired one shot at them, which missed the officers. In response, the officers fired 39 shots at Johnston. She was hit by 5 or 6 bullets. After being shot, Johnston was then handcuffed where she died minutes later in her home.

It was later discovered that one officer had planted bags of marijuana in Johnston's home after the shooting, which he admitted to later in court. The paperwork claiming the undercover officers had bought cocaine at Johnston's house prior to the shooting was later found to be forged documents. Following the investigation, the three officers involved were tried for manslaughter and other charges related to falsification. Several prosecutors claimed the Atlanta Police Department frequently lied and falsified information to gain search and arrest warrants. All three officers pleaded guilty to "conspiracy to violate civil rights, resulting in death ". They were sentenced to ten, six, and five years in prison.

Following the trial, the state senate increased restrictions on the state's no-knock warrants. Making it harder for judges to grant them and for police to obtain them. The city's police department also had to increase its warrant requirements. One year after the shooting, Johnston's family sued the city of Atlanta, the police chief, and five other officers, accusing them of false imprisonment, civil rights violations, racketeering, and other violations. The suit claims that officers used unreasonable and deadly force and that Johnston's constitutional rights against unreasonable search and seizure were violated. Johnston's family was awarded $4.9 million in a settlement.

The shooting of Kathryn Johnston is tragic for Americans. And it, like William Powell's shooting, proves that, sometimes, there isn't much standing between us and police's use of deadly force.

Given the chaotic state in which a home encounter has been found to occur. The most effective way to reduce your chances of getting shot is by practicing a combination of preventative measures. But, beyond this, it is equally important to be informed about past home encounters that have led to police shootings. It provides both mental and emotional preparation for the types of dangers that can arise in a home encounter.

The police have one essential objective: to maintain order. In a home encounter, you should keep your hands visible at all times. If you need to reach for your wallet, then tell the officer before doing so or even ask for permission. If you choose to tell the officer then you could say something along the lines of, "Officer, I am going to grab my wallet in my back pocket to show you my identification card." If you choose to ask the officer for permission, then you could say something along the lines of, "Officer, is it safe for me to reach behind my back to grab my identification?" Wait for the police officer's response before proceeding with the action. If they ask you to turn around, then obey their orders without question. The last thing you want to do in a home encounter is touch the police officer. Touching the police could result in your arrest or even a physical confrontation that may lead to the use of excessive force. The important thing to remember in any police encounter is that one thing can lead to another very quickly.

Stay Calm

It is crucial to stay calm and be respectful in a home encounter with the police. A home encounter can lead to more serious consequences if the police feel threatened by your behavior. The best thing to do in a home encounter is to be polite. If you act unreasonable, then it is likely that the police officer will act unreasonable to maintain order.

Staying calm is not an easy thing to do for people who become stressed easily. Dealing with the police at your home can easily qualify as a stressful situation. Here are some general guidelines to follow if you have trouble staying calm in stressful situations.

- **Breathe.**

Take a couple of deep breaths in and out. As you exhale, imagine the stress leaving your body.

- **Think of the big picture.**

You have to think of the big picture in a stressful encounter with the police. Is it really worth it to argue and ignore their commands even though they may seem unfounded? If you are certain there is a misunderstanding, then continue to remain calm and think of the big picture. If you live, you can always file a complaint later.

- **Put yourself in the officer's shoes.**

Putting yourself in the officer's shoes can help you stay calm in a home encounter. To do so, you will need to gauge their stress level. If the police seem very stressed and hostile, then you will need to adjust your behavior to acknowledge the situation. Not every police officer is competent and some may react poorly to a certain situation.

Showing your respect to police officers in a home encounter will lessen the chances of getting shot. If you feel threatened, it is extremely important to practice some of these tips to stay calm.

Ask If You Are Free To Leave

If you are outside when the police come to your home, then always ask if you are free to leave. Never, under any circumstance, leave before asking the police officer if you have their permission. Leaving before gaining their permission may come off as disobeying their orders and potentially get you shot in the back. If you are in a home encounter, then you could ask something as simple as, "Officer, am I free to leave?"

Know Your Rights

If you know your rights as a citizen of the United States, there will be less of a chance that a home encounter will go wrong. For one, an officer can only enter your home if you provide consent or they have a search warrant in hand. However, if you are not home when the officer arrives, they can obtain consent from a roommate or a guest if they reasonably believe that the individual has the authority to give consent.

For example, you have the right to remain silent. If you choose to remain silent, then you can say to the police, "I have the right to remain silent." You can also tell the police that you wish to speak with an attorney. If the police officer does not respect your rights, then continue to remain calm until the situation is resolved. If you feel that the officer on duty is out of line and continues to disregard your right to remain silent and right to an attorney, then take note of this and maintain your positive and diplomatic composure.

Make Sure Your Home Is Well Lit

In a police encounter at night, you will want to make sure that your home is well lit, especially any rooms they ask to walk into. Make sure to tell the officer you are going to turn on the light. A brightly lit room or front porch at night will help you take note of any details pertaining to the home encounter. It will also make yourself more visible to the officer and, thus, less likely to be viewed as a threat to the officer. Remember, police officers make decisions in just a few seconds so it is especially important to reduce your risks of being deemed as a threat to your own safety, the officer's safety, and anyone else's safety.

Pay Close Attention To Your Circumstances

In a home encounter, it is important to pay attention to the circumstances of your environment. You will want to take note of the officer's name and badge number as well as any witnesses nearby. Specifically, you will want to take note of the time of day, the police officer's questions and reason for showing up at your home. These details are very important if the officer enters your home illegally or without your permission. The more details about the encounter that you can recall will help you if you need to file a lawsuit or complaint later on.

All of these things are crucially important to be aware of in a home encounter. As we said earlier, a home encounter can happen to anyone. The best thing to do is to prepare yourself for a home encounter by being informed about your rights and aware of your external environment and the officer's statements. Also, be sure to let your hands remain visible at all times. These key guidelines will greatly reduce the chances of getting shot by the police in a home encounter.

CHAPTER 4. WALKING STOPS

Walking stops are much more common than home encounters. They often occur at night because a police officer is looking for someone or wants to know why you are on the street. If you have ever been stopped by the police, then you know how frightening it can be. Given the nature of a walk stop, it is important to understand everything you need to know about interacting with the police.

So what kind of reasons might an officer have to initiate a walk stop? One common reason is that the officer is looking for someone specific regarding a crime in the area. Police might also initiate a walk stop if they want to know why you are on the street at a certain time or place. Given the broad selection of reasons that an officer might use to stop you while walking. It is important to understand how to best respond to police questioning to reduce your chances of getting shot.

Speak Wisely

You've probably heard, the phrase "Anything you say may be used against you in a court of law" at some point. Maybe you were watching television and the officer blurted this out before they arrested a suspect.   Whatever the context in which you may have heard these words, you probably got the sense that it plays an important role in the US legal system.

If you did, then you are right. This phrase is part of the Miranda warning (also known as the Miranda rights). Police are required to say it, along with three more rights, to criminal suspects before they are questioned to preserve the admissibility of their statements against them in a court of law.

What does it mean for you in a walk stop? You need to really consider what you say to the police, because they can use it against you later. It can also give the police reason to arrest you. Refrain from badmouthing the police or making threats that can be used against you in court. Often times, it is best to wait to speak until you reach a safer destination such as the police station. By following the police's orders, you remove yourself from a more dangerous situation— even if they are wrong or you are innocent.

Identify Yourself

If the police are looking for someone in particular, then you may be asked to show your identification. In many states, you have no legal obligation to show the police your identification in a walk stop. However, there are exceptions to this rule. If the police have properly detained you, they may also ask for your full name. If you refuse to give the police your full name, some states allow the police to arrest you. Let's say that you have an incriminating name. In this case, you can claim your right to remain silent. However, although you may have certain rights, if there is no reason to withhold your personal information from the police it is highly recommended that you comply with all reasonable requests. Compliance can show the police that you are truly not a threat to the public safety and their own. Thus, while we always urge citizens to practice their rights, we also urge citizens to proceed with caution and assess their specific situation appropriately.

Consent or Not

The police must have your consent to search you. Consenting to a search can impact your rights in court. If the police claim they have a search warrant, then you should ask to see it. Remember, you must remain calm throughout all of this. Remember, your number one priority in a walk stop is to not get shot by the police.

Do Not Resist

If you are in a walk stop with the police, it is crucially important to not resist the officer. Even if they wrongfully detain or arrest you on false grounds, you should never physically resist the officer. Instead, pay attention to every detail of the situation and what the officer specifically says to you before conducting a nonconsensual search.

General Tips For Walk Stops

A walk stop can often lead to your arrest if you act suspiciously or fail to comply with the officer's reasonable requests. So here are some things you want to keep in mind during a walk stop:

- Watch what you say as well as your body language and emotions.
- Do not argue with the police.
- Anything you say or do can be used against you in a court of law.
- Make sure your hands and arms are visible to the police.
- Never run.
- Never touch the police.
- Never threaten the police.
- Do not resist (even if you are innocent).
- Do not tell the police they are wrong.
- Choose your right to remain silent.
- Request that you speak to a lawyer.
- Take note of officer names, badge numbers, and patrol car numbers.
- Document everything you can remember about the situation as soon as you can.
- Take note of any witnesses and get their names and contact information.
- Document any injuries from the walk stop immediately.
- Try to reduce baggy clothes or jackets that will cause police suspicion during a walk stop.

These are some of the most helpful guidelines to keep in mind during a walk stop. Especially, the fact that there will almost always be a witness or a nearby camera on public sidewalks or areas with heavy foot traffic. Remain calm during a walk stop and follow your best judgment even when you have certain rights available to you. Often times, practicing your rights during a walk stop can lead to harsh force. Thus, it is always good to practice compliance and respect when dealing with the police.

CHAPTER 5. CAR STOPS

The car stop is also one of the most common ways to get shot by the police. If you have follow the news, you probably know the name Philando Castle. His death in a car stop has stirred national controversy over police shootings after the encounter was caught on a live video and posted to Facebook.

The incident took place in Falcon Heights, Minnesota in July. In the video, a woman in the car is heard saying, "We got pulled over for a busted tail light in the back." The woman turns the camera to Castile, who is bleeding in a white t-shirt. The officer can be seen outside the car window with his gun drawn. The woman tells the officer that Castile is licensed to carry a firearm. The officer shot Philando after he was reaching for his Identification at the request of the officer.

The woman remained calm for the majority of the incident. On the other hand, the officer outside the car window yelled expletives. After the officer asks her to step outside of the vehicle with her hands up in the air, the woman obeys and begins to walk backwards with the camera pointed at the police. The woman maintained her composure up until the camera is thrown onto the ground. She began to cry and plead with the officers. Once being detained in the police cruiser, the woman resumes her calm demeanor.

The video has since been removed from Facebook, but while it was up, we learned a few things that the woman, Diamond Reynolds, did correctly in the car stop.

For one, she remained calm throughout the majority of the situation even after Castile was shot dead by the police officer. Doing so reduced the chances of her being shot by the police as well. The situation demonstrates the manner in which a car stop can go horribly wrong within a matter of seconds.

Even if you don't get shot by the police, you may still suffer other consequences. Take, for example, a recent car stop in New Mexico that resulted in a man suing the city of Deming for being forced to undergo an anal cavity search, three enemas, and a colonoscopy.

The man, David Eckert, was stopped during a routine traffic stop and asked to step out of his car. Eckert was holding his legs together with an erect posture and the officer thought he was holding drugs. The police got a search warrant but did not get permission to use medical procedures for an anal cavity search. After being taken a nearby hospital, the doctors found no drugs hidden inside Eckert.

Although Eckert had to endure an invasion of privacy, be humiliated and had his manhood stripped, it should be noted that the incident serves as another demonstration of how one man was able to avoid getting shot by the police during a car stop. It should also be noted that Eckert later sued and local authorities settled with him for $1.6 million dollars.

Know Your Rights In A Car Stop

You need to know your rights in a car stop. They happen all of the time and if you drive a vehicle, then it is likely you will be pulled over at some point in your life. So pay close attention to your rights so you can be prepared for a car stop.

The first right you should know about is that police officers must have probable cause to pull you over. They cannot simply look at you and search your vehicle for drugs. As was the case in Castile's incident, police officers must have a reason to pull you over such as a broken tail light. You also do not have to pull over until it is safe to do so. However, if it is unsafe to pull over you must notify the police officer with a hand signal and you will want to pull over as soon as possible to not upset the officer.

As a citizen, you have the right to remain in your car, although it looks bad to some officers. Getting out of the car when asked to do so could make the situation less tense than if you were to refuse. You can also refuse to be tested with a breathalyzer in many states. For example, in New York, drivers have the right to refuse a breathalyzer test under the statute, "implied consent." However, other states will automatically suspend your license if you refuse the test. And if the police officer suspects you of drug use or DUI, then they have probable cause to give you a blood test at the police station.

Drivers should also be aware that they have to stop at checkpoints. You can be sure that driving away from a police checkpoint without stopping is grounds for probable cause and could lead to getting shot by the cops.

Many of you may be wondering about your rights during a car search. It is often assumed that police officers must have a warrant to do so, which is usually the case. There are five exceptions to this rule. The first one is perhaps the most obvious of them all, which is that police can search your car if you give them consent. The second exception is called "plain view," which is when, for example, a bag of drugs is explicitly visible and the police officer notices it without having to search your car. If something is in plain view, the officer does not need a warrant to search the rest of your car. Under the "search incident to arrest," an officer can arrest you with probable cause and then proceed to search your vehicle without a warrant. The police may also search your car if the "officer has probable cause to suspect a crime." Thus, if your front seat has blood on it and you have bruises all over your knuckles, then the police officer may suspect a crime. The fifth exception is called "exigent circumstances," which is when an officer suspects that any evidence is about to be destroyed before getting a search warrant.

If an officer suspects something and obtains a warrant to search your car, then you MUST obey. Knowing your rights in a car stop is great, but unless you know what to do to avoid getting shot by the police all of this information is pretty much useless.

Pull Over Quickly

We briefly mentioned earlier that pulling over quickly is a good idea. It's also important to pull over safely. By pulling over quickly and safely, you are acknowledging the police officer's attempt to speak with you.

Remember to use your turn signals and drive the speed limit. You can also be near the area where the officer believes you broke the law, which gives you the advantage of seeing the scene for yourself and describe the situation in detail.

Do Not Reach For ANYTHING!

As soon as you are stopped, you will want to make sure your hands are visible to the officer. Do not tuck them under your legs. Instead, keep them firmly placed on both sides of the steering wheel (10 o'clock and 2 o'clock). Roll your window down (*all of them if they are tinted*) and then turn off your engine. All of these steps will make it clear to the officer that you have no plans to drive off or grab a weapon. If you are pulled over in the dark, then make sure to turn on all of your interior lights. Most importantly, do not reach for anything. Even if you are trying to pull out your documentation or license, the officer is trained to react quickly to any potential threat. He or she does not know that you are simply reaching for your registration or license and such an act is likely to be misinterpreted by the officer.

Check Your Behavior

An officer will be sure to search your car if they suspect suspicious behavior. Make sure you aren't hunched down in your seat, because the officer might think you are hiding something under your seat. Of course, you might have picked up on this one earlier, but do not keep your legs shut together. You want to sit upright in your seat and be natural. These rules do not solely apply to criminals. They apply to everyone. Time and time again, police officers misinterpret an individual's actions and, unwilling to take the risk, they make a quick decision to eliminate the threat or to escalate the car stop.

Only Get Out Of The Car If Asked

Getting out of the car on your own is going to come off as aggressive and threatening to the police officer. It is likely that the officer will interpret you getting out of the car as an attempt to flee the scene or fight. On the other hand, if the officer does ask you to get out of your vehicle, then do so calmly without making any sudden movements.

Speak When Asked To Speak

Speaking too much or too little could cause a car stop to quickly escalate into getting shot by the police. If you are in a traffic stop, be sure to only speak when asked to speak. For example, if the officer asks you a question, then respond with a clear answer. The police officer will likely ask you, "Do you know why I pulled you over?" When the officer asks you to answer a question like this, it means they are encouraging you to incriminate yourself by permitting you to confess to violations. You can give noncommittal responses or remain silent. Giving an answer you may think is likely only gives the officer a reason when you might have done nothing wrong.

So, if you find yourself in a traffic stop with the police, then remember to pull over quickly and safely, roll your window down (*all of them if they are tinted),* shut your engine off and keep your hands on the steering wheel (10 o'clock and 2 o'clock). When the officer gets to your window, make sure to be polite, think before you speak, and let the officer do the talking.

CHAPTER 6. CONSENSUAL STOPS

A consensual encounter is one of three categories of Fourth Amendment police-citizen interaction. The Fourth Amendment states,

"Amendment IV – The right of the people to be secure in their persons, houses, papers and effects, against unreasonable searches and seizures, shall not be violated, and no Warrants shall issue, but upon probable cause, supported by Oath or affirmation, and particularly describing the place to be searched, and the persons or things to be seized."

The other two types of police interactions are detentions and arrests. During a consensual encounter the police use no commands, force, or sirens. Instead, the police officer will approach you in conversation and, thus, need no level of justification to do so.

During a consensual encounter, the police can legally speak with you without any cause for suspicion. These types of encounters often begin with the police officer saying something along the lines of, "Would you mind talking with me for a minute?" You have the right to not speak with the officer and you can leave at any time. If the officer is on your property you have the right to ask them to leave. Instead of being rude, you can suggest, "I'm sorry officer, but I'm already late for an appointment and I can't talk right now."

Just because an officer initiates a conversation with you does not mean they do not suspect you of committing a crime. If an officer confronts you in a consensual encounter, they may just lack the proper evidence. They may also be trying to get you to say something that can be used against you.

You should also know that the police have no obligation to read your Miranda rights before engaging in a consensual encounter. In other words, consenting to a consensual encounter means that whatever you say or do can be used against you in a court of law.

Here's what you need to know: a consensual encounter can give the police reasonable suspicion to escalate the situation into an investigative detention.

The Danger Of A Consensual Stop

On the books, a consensual encounter seems like a very straightforward situation about which to worry. We hate to be the bearer of bad news, but consensual stops are by no means straightforward nor something to put you at ease.

Back in 2011, Joseph June was riding his bicycle down the Gulf Coast Highway in Florida when Officer Jason Von Ansbach Young pulled up behind him in a cruiser. Young got out of the cruiser and started talking with June. According to Young, he initiated a consensual encounter with Young because he wanted to make an acquaintance. Like many others would, June got nervous during the consensual encounter. He started fidgeting because he had a pocketknife on him.

The police officer deemed June's fidgeting as enough justification to conduct a search. June's fate got much worse. Young found a bag of cocaine in June's shirt, which is a third-degree felony in Florida.

To make matters worse, the 64-year-old African American man already had a lifelong history of criminal activity. The consensual encounter resulted in June receiving the maximum sentence of five years in prison.

In a court of law, June argued that Young undertook an illegal stop-and-frisk, but Judge Joseph Lewis denied his allegations and determined Young's actions to have been in line with protocol. He had stopped to talk with June and used his suspicious behavior as reason to search him.

So, what does all of this have to do with not getting shot by the police?

June's story is a classic example of how police use consensual encounters as a way to escalate a situation without an explicit probable cause. In New York City, a stop-and-frisk works the same way as it does in Florida, only there's way more of them. In 2011 alone, there were 685,724 police stops; 605,328 of which resulted in the police finding nothing.

The problem with the stop-and-frisk is that it's the police officer's word against yours. Consensual encounters highly favor the police officer, especially if they find something during a search. The bigger problem is that the consensual encounter gives the police the power to stop anyone for anything. Also, their criteria for suspicion is extremely subjective and often out of your control.

The consensual encounter has the effect of blurring the police officer's real intention for stopping you. If you are like most people, then you would probably get pretty nervous if a police officer were to just walk up to you and start talking without a clear motive.

Consensual Encounters Gone Wrong

A consensual encounter is often the precursor for a police shooting. One such example of a consensual encounter gone wrong is the police shooting of an unarmed, mentally ill, African American man Ezell Ford in 2015. The incident occurred in Los Angeles. After two officers watched Ford walking away from a group of gang members and saw him put his hands in his pocket, they decided to initiate a consensual encounter with Ford. The officers said Ford walked away very quickly as the officers approached. Ford was shot three times by both officers after they claimed he lunged towards one of their guns. However, it was later determined that one officer had inappropriately drawn his gun but was justified in his use of excessive force.

What To Do During A Consensual Encounter

If you find yourself in a consensual encounter, then make sure to act natural. Don't get uptight and nervous because it could cause the police officer to suspect you of a crime you didn't commit.

Many people typically have a negative attitude towards the police, but during a consensual encounter it is important to remember that your number one priority is your life. Expressing your opinion towards an officer of the law during a consensual encounter could lead to a much worse situation. That being said, do not make any threats or demeaning gestures towards the officer. You can simply smile and go on your own way after explaining to the officer that you cannot talk at this time.

Running from the scene without saying anything may come off as a reason to believe you are guilty for something. The same goes for profuse sweating, nervous talking, or frantic movements.

How To Avoid A Consensual Stop

Some consider consensual encounters an example of a Legal Fiction. A legal fiction refers to something that is only legally true for the sake of convenience, but isn't true in reality.

This perspective argues that you don't really consent in a consensual encounter, because consenting suggests that you have a choice in a particular situation. But in a police consensual encounter, do you really have a choice? Let's say that you're walking on the street, minding your own business, and then a police officer walks up to you to ask who you are and why you're walking on the street. We have to be real with ourselves here for a moment. In a situation like this, do you really have the power to say that you can't talk and want to be left alone? The police might take this as a reason to suspect you of being guilty and stop you anyway.

Despite the reality of the situation, the law would consider this to be a consensual encounter. It's the police officer's word against yours and whatever they provide as a reason for suspicion will be used against you in a court of law. The problem is that the government fails to consider the weight of "pragmatics," which refers to how the meaning of words change based on context. Legally speaking, most judges will consider an officer's question as a command.

A consensual encounter can be a sticky situation, so here's some ways to avoid them all together:

1. Just say no

You can start off by denying an officer's desire to initiate a consensual encounter. While there is no telling how far this will get you in a police consensual stop, the less you say, the less that can be used against you in a court of law. If you choose to not give your consent to a police encounter, it is probably a good idea to consider the politest way to do it. For example, you could say something like, "Hello officer, I appreciate your offer to speak with me but I will have to politely decline. I hope you have a good day." Saying something as polite and formal as this can be unrealistic in certain situations. Although there may not be one true answer to this question, it helps to know the weight of your words.

2. Get serious

If you are still being pressed to engage in a consensual police encounter, then you can get seriously polite. Use whatever excuse you can but make sure it makes sense and it doesn't make you appear as a guilty criminal. Change your tone of voice to an easy going and friendly one if the officer begins to grow angry. Whatever you do, it is important to never respond to an officer's frustration with more frustration. Finally, if it gets really serious, you can explicitly state that you refuse to give your consent to a consensual police encounter. If you choose to do this, remember the officer's name and badge number or squad car number. Remember—do not make any sudden movements. Walk away calmly and give no reason for suspicion.

3. Give Consent

Most of you out there are law-abiding citizens with little reason to avoid a consensual encounter. If you fall into this category, you should ask yourself, "Is there really any reason that I should take my chances and deny consent?" More than likely, there is not a reason for you to deny your consent if the police officer is genuinely seeking help for an investigation or a 911 phone call. It will be subtly clear to you if the police officer mistakenly suspects you of committing a crime and is attempting to escalate the situation into an arrest. If the police officer does not appear to be trying to incriminate you, then giving your consent is your best option. After all, denying your consent will almost always appear as suspicious by most police officers and could quickly escalate the situation.

CHAPTER 7. COMMUNITY CARETAKER STOPS

In a community caretaker encounter the police have a reasonable cause to believe you are in need of their assistance. A community caretaker stop could happen if you are sleeping in your car, for example. The police may ask something along the lines of, "Hey there, are you okay?" Other examples of a community caretaker situation may involve medical-related issues such as a stroke or heart attack. Many of these community caretaker stops can quickly escalate into a severe situation if the officer has reasonable cause to suspect you of a crime.

One instance of a "community caretaker encounter" gone wrong was the shooting of Trayvon Martin, a 17-year-old African American high school student. On February 26, 2012, Martin was shot by George Zimmerman, a 28-year-old Hispanic man, in Sanford Florida. Zimmerman was the neighborhood watch coordinator for a gated community where Martin was living where the shooting took place.

The man shot unarmed Martin roughly two minutes before the police arrived. He was released after the police questioned him for five hours, because there was no evidence to go against Zimmerman's claim of self-defense.

However, the story rapidly spread around the country and fueled protests that called for Zimmerman's arrest and further investigation. Six weeks after the shooting, Zimmerman was arrested and charged with murder by a prosecutor appointed by Governor Rick Scott. Zimmerman's trial took place on July 13, 2013. The jury acquitted him. On February 24, 2015, the United States Department of Justice stated, "There was not enough evidence for a federal hate crime prosecution."

Although Trayvon Martin was shot by a civilian rather than a police officer, it is important to acknowledge the similarities between Zimmerman's actions and community caretaker encounters. During Zimmerman's phone call to the police, he is heard disregarding the dispatcher's directions to remain inside his SUV upon seeing a "suspicious person" in his community. Soon after Zimmerman left his SUV to confront Martin, the neighbors reported hearing the sound of gunshots.

How To Avoid A Community Caretaker Encounter

Avoiding a community caretaker encounter is a little bit easier than avoiding a consensual police encounter. That being said, it's not always straightforward and you should use your best judgment to determine the smartest solution for your particular situation.

Let's say an officer knocks on your window after they notice you're slumped over the steering wheel. They might think you're intoxicated, but in reality, you're just trying to work up the energy to get of your car and walk inside your house. If it is clear to the officer that you are not intoxicated, then you can try to avoid the encounter by acknowledging that you are safe and do not require their assistance. After doing so, simply ask the officer if you are free to go.

If the police officer denies your request to leave, it means the situation is no longer a community caretaker stop and you are suspected of violating the law. We hope that none of our readers ever have to endure wrongful accusations or misunderstandings with the police, because it can lead to erroneous decision making by both involved parties. However, if you do find yourself in this particular situation, be sure to show compliance.

What Counts As A Community Caretaker Stop?

The police can undertake a community caretaker stop in a variety of situations. Some examples may include:

- Checking on the drivers parked in rest areas, especially if the weather is bad.
- Opening a vehicle door if the officer is concerned for the driver's life.
- Pulling over a motorist with an unsafe motorcycle helmet.
- Informing a driver about dangerous road conditions in the area.
- Pulling over a motorist for having a large object (usually furniture) hanging out the back of their vehicle.
- Observing a motorist driving far under the speed limit with their emergency lights on.

On the other hand, there are a couple of known situations in which a community caretaker stop is Not permitted. These include:

- Stopping a driver that is legally parked in an area where young people often consume alcohol.
- Informing a driver about a particular regulation or concern that was asked weeks ago.
- Seeing a driver sit at a stop sign for 45-60 seconds and drive away (at an appropriate speed) upon seeing the police cruiser.

Being an informed citizen is vital during a police encounter. If we understand the conditions in which a police officer can engage in a community caretaker encounter, then we will have an increased chance of staying alive by knowing how to diffuse a situation. Furthermore, if we understand why a police officer might stop us and engage in a community caretaker encounter, it may prevent rash decisions from being made. Peoples' natural nerves often lead them to panic and assume they are being stopped for something far worse. Scenarios play out in our heads as the police approach us and we may act suspiciously as a result. Suspicious behavior could lead the officer to believe, for example, you are reaching for a weapon when, in reality, you may be simply trying to grab identification from your back pocket. However, if we are aware of the situations in which a community caretaker encounter is permitted, we may be able to keep calm during exchanges with the police. The point is, that our behavior is less likely to appear suspicious to police officers if we are well-informed of the particular situations in which they can initiate a community caretaker encounter.

That being said, Trayvon Martin's situation is one example of how these things alone may not be enough to prevent you from being shot by a community watch member, like Zimmerman.

Prior to shooting Martin, Zimmerman had called the police several times to report what he believed to be "suspicious people" in his community. During each phone call, Zimmerman only offered information about their race. Zimmerman told the dispatcher the individuals were black males. When Zimmerman called the police about Trayvon Martin, he stated, "We've had some break-ins in my neighborhood, and there's a real suspicious guy." He said Martin was "just walking around looking about" in the rain and said, "This guy looks like he is up to no good or he is on drugs or something." Zimmerman also told the police the person had his hand in his waistband and was walking nearby homes. According to Zimmerman, Martin began to run. The dispatcher told Zimmerman to not follow suit after he said, "these assholes, always get away" and followed Martin anyway. Martin was attempting to go inside his home when Zimmerman shot him outside the rear door of the townhouse where he was staying.

Exception To The Fourth Amendment

The community caretaker encounter is often exempt from the Fourth Amendment's prohibition against warrantless searches. For example, if your home is burning down, then an officer has permission to enter the home if they have reason to believe someone's life is in danger. Other situations may include hearing gunshots inside a home or noticing a clearly broken window or front door. That being said, every situation is different and there is no clear and definitive set of rules that qualify as an exemption to a warrantless search.

More often than not, you will probably be grateful for the police's intervention if you are in true danger. Yet, there are still several situations in which a community caretaker stop could be a violation of your Fourth Amendment right and potentially lead to the use of excessive force.

Overall, a consensual encounter is a gray area in the legal world. That being said, you should take precautions just as you would in a home encounter, traffic stop, or a walk stop and place your safety above all else.

Chapter 8. Know Your Rights

We have talked about your rights in various police encounter situations but it is important to really know them, which is why this entire chapter is devoted to citizens' rights in a police encounter.

DUI Checkpoints

DUI checkpoints are also known as sobriety checkpoints. If you haven't encountered a sobriety checkpoint, then it's exactly what it sounds like. The police set up DUI checkpoints to catch drunk drivers and they are the most common type of roadblock. They're usually quick and give the police enough time to check tags and license plate numbers. The police will typically try and smell your breath as well as briefly look at the inside of your vehicle to determine if you have been drinking or have an open bottle of alcohol in the open.

At a DUI checkpoint, the police do not have the right to search your vehicle unless they have probable cause that you are drinking and driving or you consent to a search. You also have the right to remain silent during a DUI checkpoint. Many police departments will have drug-sniffing dogs at roadblocks. More than likely, you will be unable to evade a police checkpoint and trying to do so would likely cause suspicion.

US Border Checkpoints

Customs and Border Protection agents work with the Department of Homeland Security and they do not need probable cause or a warrant to search you, your belongings or your vehicle at the border. In other words, crossing the border is the equivalent of giving your consent to a search.

The agents are allowed to use pat-down, strip, body cavity, or involuntary x-ray methods to undertake the search.

However, if you have a laptop, for example, the Ninth Circuit Court of Appeals now require border agents to have probable cause to conduct a search of your electronic devices. The ruling still allows border agents to open your laptop to take a quick look at the windows you have open. You do not have to voluntarily give the agents any passwords to your personal files, computer, mobile phone, and so on.

The Homeland Security Department also have security checkpoints up to 100 miles inside the United States. If you encounter one of these security roadblocks, you do not need to answer any questions. You also have the right to deny your consent to any searches.

Drug Checkpoints

Although the Supreme Court recently ruled random checkpoints with the intent to find illegal drugs as unconstitutional, the police often find ways to set drug checkpoints up anyway.

The police are still allowed to place warning signs for drug checkpoints. They cannot pull anyone that passes through the checkpoint over, but they will observe vehicles approaching the nonexistent checkpoint and pull over drivers who make illegal turns to evade the police. They will also look for individuals who attempt to throw away any contraband before arriving at the checkpoint.

Since technically these checkpoints do not actually exist, drivers should just continue to drive without trying to evade them. If the signs are placed right before a rest area, it is also a good idea to not pull into it. The police may suspect you of throwing away contraband or attempting to wait out the imaginary drug checkpoint.

TSA Checkpoints

As a branch of the Department of Homeland Security, the Transportation Security Administration (TSA) has the right to search you and your belongings without a warrant or probable cause. That is, if you are passing through a TSA airport security zone.

At Home

If the police show up at your home, then you should be aware of your rights because there are quite a few. Most notably, is the need for a search warrant. The police cannot search your home under the 4th amendment without probable cause or a search warrant signed by a judge. However, if you give the officer consent to search your home, then the officers do not need to obtain a warrant nor do they need to have probable cause. Giving consent to an officer to come inside your home permits them to seize anything in plain view as evidence. This can also lead to a quick arrest or escalate the situation if you have dangerous weapons in your home. That being said, you will want to keep your private items tucked away, which is just a good idea to begin with.

You do not have to let the police inside. You can speak to the police outside and shut your door to avoid a forced entry. You can also speak to the officers with a chain lock on the door. If the police are at your home and you do not need their assistance, then you can ask them to leave.

Your Miranda Rights

A lot of people wrongly believe that a police officer is required to read you your Miranda rights during an arrest. Sorry, folks, but that's not actually the case. On the contrary, the police only have to read a person his or her Miranda rights if they are placed under arrest and if you are about to be questioned about a crime. If you, for example, were to give an officer your consent to have your home searched and they find drugs for which you claim responsibility, then the police do not have any legal obligation to read the Miranda rights.

The police also have no legal obligation to inform you that you can refuse searches without a warrant or probable cause. In fact, many police officers may attempt to make it seem as if you are legally obligated to do so through intimidation tactics. The police can obtain your oral consent to conduct a search and do not need to have it in writing.

The best thing to do during a police arrest is to claim your right to remain silent and speak to an attorney.

Non-US Citizens

Even if you are not a citizen of the United States, you are still protected under the 4th amendment.

Non-citizens include lawful permanent residents, refugees, and asylum seekers as well as anyone with permission to come to the United States for work, school, or travel. Non-citizens also include individuals who do not have legal immigration status. Generally, all individuals that lack legal immigration status share the same constitutional rights as citizens for police stops, questionings, arrests, and searches.

However, there are several exceptions to these rules. For one, if you are a non-citizen trying to cross the border and enter the U.S., you do not have the same rights.

The police or other types of law enforcement officers may ask you questions about your background, immigration status, relatives and colleagues. However, in order for the police to ask any of these questions, they must obtain your consent. In other words, as a non-citizen you have the right to remain silent unless you are in an airport or a border.

You also have no legal obligation to answer questions about your birthplace, home, or U.S. citizenship. In fact, you will want to speak with a lawyer before answering any questions about your immigration status.

Non-immigrants include all non-citizens who are authorized to be in the United States. Generally, non-immigrants share the same rights as citizens with one notable exception. The police can require non-immigrants to provide information on their immigration status.

Although you might not necessarily have to show the police your immigration documents, it is often a good idea to do so. By law, all non-citizens over the age of 18 must carry valid US immigration documents with them (if they have them). You might know these as "alien registration." Refusing to show the police these documents can lead to an arrest or worse if the situation gets out of hand. It is always best to take the highest level of precautions as possible during a police encounter to reduce your chances of being shot.

Search Warrants

If an officer presents a warrant to search your home, you have the right to review it for accuracy. The warrant is a piece of paper with a signature from a judge that permits the police to enter and search your home or other building as well as make an arrest if they discover adequate grounds to do so during the search. The warrant should describe the place they plan to search as well as what they plan to look for such as specific items.

A search warrant should show the judge's name, your name, address, the date, place to be searched, a description of items being searched for, and the name of the organization conducting the search or arrest. In some circumstances, a search warrant is still valid even if it does not include your name. If the warrant is able to list the correct address and describe the place to be searched, then the warrant is still credible.

Arrest Warrant

An arrest warrant is different than a search warrant. With an arrest warrant, the police have permission to take you into custody, but it does not give them the right to search your home. If the police come to your home to arrest you, they can only look in areas where they suspect you to be hiding. They can also take evidence that is in plain sight, but they cannot, for example, go through filing cabinets.

An arrest warrant does not require your name to be present on the form if it is able to describe you in enough detail to make an accurate identification.

If you are presented with a paper that says something along the lines of "warrant of deportation/removal," then know that this is an entirely different type of warrant that does not grant the same permissions to enter or search a building or make an arrest.

Investigative Detention

Earlier we discussed the consensual police encounter, which is one of three tiers of police encounters. An investigative detention is the second type of police encounter, which is when the police temporarily detain a citizen for further questioning. In order to place you under investigative detention, the police are required to have reasonable articulable suspicion. Some of the potential reasons for suspicion include crowbars, slim jims, weapons, spray paint cans, rolling papers, plastic sandwich bags, scales, and pipes. Police will also look for warning signs such as paper tags, police decals, college attire and gangster attire. The police will detain you for around 20 minutes at most. During an investigative detention encounter, you are not free to leave until the police say so. You also have no legal obligation to show your ID to the police officers in 26 states.

Arrest

An arrest is the third tier of police encounters and it occurs when the police take a citizen into custody. An arrest is obviously the worst kind of police encounter you can get involved in. The police are required to have probable cause or a warrant to conduct an arrest. Sometimes it isn't always clear as to whether or not the officer is placing you under arrest. You have the right to ask, "Am I under arrest?" The police officer must answer this question and indicate whether you are under arrest or not. If you are under arrest, you are required by law to show your ID. Refusing to show your ID during an arrest is a horrible idea and could lead to the use of excessive force. Regarding your rights during an arrest search, the police are entitled to frisk you and collect any evidence in plain sight. However, they are still required to get your consent or a warrant to search your vehicle. If you are immediately arrested, it is likely that the police caught you in the act of committing a crime. If you are caught committing a crime, you should be extremely cooperative and compliant with the officers because it is almost certain that the police consider you to be a threat. In other words, the police will take much less risks in an arrest situation and will be more likely to shoot you for any sudden movement, abnormal behavior or threats. It is important to note that getting caught with a weapon can significantly escalate an arrest and lead to you getting shot by the police. If you do survive an arrest with a deadly weapon, then you should be aware of the legal consequences for illegal weapon carry. Basically, all you need to know is that if you are caught committing a crime, arrested, and the police discover you are carrying a weapon, your sentence will be much more severe if you didn't have one. The bottom line is, during an arrest, only tell the officer your name. Anything else could escalate the situation. If you have reason to believe you were wrongfully arrested, you can calmly address this with the officer but refrain from getting into an argument. If you know the officer violated your rights during your arrest it is almost always better to wait to address these concerns with a lawyer or in a safe environment where the police officer is certain that you have no access to weapons.

Other Important Rights

With the recent controversies surrounding the deaths of Michael Brown and Eric Garner , more and more Americans are requesting information about their rights in a variety of situations. So pay close attention to some of the following scenarios in which you could be arrested for being unaware of what rights you have and do not have.

1. Refusing to leave

If a police officer orders you to leave the premises (public or private), then you may be arrested. Whether or not the officer can legally arrest you for not leaving an area depends on the reason. For example, if you are disrupting traffic by sitting in the middle of the road, then the officer can arrest you for refusing to leave. Many protestor arrests are a result of disrupting traffic. Furthermore, if you are on private property without permission, you may also be arrested for refusing to leave. Besides this, if you are breaking the law in any way, the police have enough reason to arrest you for refusing to vacate the premises. However, if the police order you to leave a public space simply because they disagree with your message, then they have no right to arrest you for refusing to leave. If you find yourself in this situation you should know that police officers will likely be upset if they disagree with your message and will do whatever they can to find a reason to arrest you. Such encounters can quickly escalate and call for the use of excessive force. While you may care deeply about a particular issue and want to practice your right to freedom of speech, ultimately, you have to acknowledge that "to live and die another day" will be beneficial to your cause.

When I said that the police will typically try to find any way to arrest you for refusing to leave on public property, I was largely referencing the plentiful regulations of public roadways. If you plan to participate or initiate a protest in a public space, then you should read up on your local laws regarding public roadways since these can get very specific and change from city to city. You will want to search for anything that pertains to traffic jams or pedestrian safety. Generally, it is legal to congregate on the sidewalk and illegal to do so on the road where you would be blocking traffic.

2. Recording a police encounter

With the mass amount of videos of police encounters posted to Facebook and YouTube, you have probably wondered if it's illegal to do so. Many officers express their distaste towards citizens who record police encounters and ask that they turn off their camera. The answer is that it is generally legal to record an on-duty police officer in the public arena. However, there are some state laws that limit your rights in this regard. Furthermore, you should be aware that the police have the right to arrest you if they feel you are obstructing an investigation by recording a situation with your phone. Generally speaking, if you are in a "reasonable distance" that doesn't interfere with the police doing their job, you should be fine.

3. Curfews

The police do have the right to put curfews into effect. Situations that would call for a curfew include any type of emergency situation. The police put curfews into effect to protect the lives, safety, and property of civilians. Although the police have a significant amount of authority regarding public curfews, there are some instances where a curfew can be deemed unconstitutional. A curfew is considered unconstitutional if the police put it in effect only to obstruct a peaceful gathering.

4. Car stops

If you are pulled over for a traffic violation the police are entitled to see your license, vehicle registration, and proof of insurance. However, you are not required to answer questions.

5. Right to a lawyer

The right to a lawyer is a fundamental constitutional right that every police officer will be aware of. The police may not inform you that you have this right, but just remember that it applies to every situation in which the police may attempt to question you. The purpose of a lawyer is to protect your rights as a civilian. If you tell an officer that you want to speak to your lawyer and exercise your right to remain silent, the officer should cease any questions. If they continue to ask questions, then you can restate your right to remain silent. You do not need to already have a lawyer to request to speak to one. If you do have a lawyer it is a good idea to carry their contact information with you to show the police officer and request to call them. Your lawyer will want to know the officer's name, badge number, patrol car number, and any other relevant information about your encounter with the police. Even if you begin to answer some questions, you have the right to refuse to answer anything you do not wish to. Lastly, the police cannot listen to your conversation with your lawyer. However, they can listen to any phone calls you make to anyone else such as family, friends, or associates.

6. The grand jury subpoena

An officer of the law might try to intimidate you with a grand jury subpoena, which is a written order for you to go to court and spill any information about a particular situation. Even if the police officer threatens you with a grand jury subpoena, you still have the right to remain silent. If the situation escalates to this point, then you should call a lawyer as soon as possible. If the officer gets the subpoena, you should follow the directions and report to court accordingly.

7. Right to refuse a counter-terrorism interview

If the police ask you to participate in a counter-terrorism interview, you have the right to refuse to be interviewed. You also have the right to have an attorney present at the interview if you choose to do so and schedule the time and place of the interview. Additionally, you have the right to know all of the questions the police intend to ask you before the interview. You are not required to answer all of the questions.

8. Right to deny consent for a search

You have the right to deny your consent for a search and the officer cannot use this as a reason for probable cause. All grounds for probable cause or reasonable suspicion must be based on concrete facts. These include, for example, a criminal history or being in possession of evidence of a crime.

9. Right to ask for officer's identifying information

If you feel that you were treated poorly by an officer of the law, then you have the right to request their identifying information such as their name, badge number Etc.

10. Office searches

The police may only search your office with a warrant or with the consent of your employer regardless if you provide consent.

Take-Aways

Often times, a consensual encounter or an investigative detention will escalate into an arrest. That being said, start small and work your way up. Know that lying to an officer of the law is a criminal offense. Also know that anything you say can and will be used against you in a court of law. Understanding your rights for a consensual encounter will greatly reduce your chances of being involved in an investigative detention or a police arrest.

It is crucially important that you take the initiative to explore your specific state and local laws regarding police encounters. None of this information should be considered professional legal guidance. Ultimately, it is your job to understand which rights apply to you according to your specific state, city, and county.

In 1999, four plain clothed New York City police officers Edward McMellon, Sean Carroll, Kenneth Boss and Richard Murphy shot an unarmed 23-year-old immigrant Amadou Diallo 41 times as he was reaching for his wallet. Officer Kenneth Boss had been previously involved in an incident where another unarmed man was shot and killed just two years earlier. The officers claim they thought Diallo was reaching for a gun. A Bronx grand jury indicted the four officers on charges of second-degree murder and reckless endangerment. On February 25, 2000, after two days of deliberation, a jury in Albany, New York acquitted the officers of all charges. Diallo's family filed a Lawsuit against city and officers for $61 million: they later settled for $3 million.

The tragic situation is another example of how the fate of citizens in police shootings is dependent on the officer's perspective. If the police officer senses a high level of danger in a specific situation and can provide factual evidence to justify these beliefs, then it is reasonable to believe that the officer made the best decision given the circumstances.

Thus, in the midst of national debate over the extent to which police officers take responsibility for their actions on-duty, the perspective of the police is important to understand to reduce your chances of getting shot. Whether you agree or disagree with the way police are punished or unpunished for their actions, we must all acknowledge the fact that our lives are in their hands. Thus, if we want to live, we should try to understand the police psyche.

Decision Making

The police are expected to make a split decision within a matter of seconds. A recent study by Washington State University Spokane revealed that white AND black officers are more biased against African American suspects. This maybe due to racism or down right fear based on images they've seen in the media.

Some officers however, are more hesitant to shoot African American suspects due to the recent backlash from the public arena and fear of being labeled racist.

The data was collected through a police-training simulator that teaches officers how to address a potentially deadly encounter. During one scenario, a simulated suspect fired at the officer who returned fire. In only 1.1 seconds, the suspect fired two times and the officer fired four shots. In another simulation, a citizen tried the simulator. He was told to use deadly force in response to a suspect in connection with an assault. Within a matter of seconds, the civilian shot the suspect after he reached for what was later discovered to be a beer bottle.

It is relatively easy to imagine the level of stress on police officers during hostile situations. While it may not account for all of the police shootings in recent months, it does explain some of them in which police officers reasonably believed a suspect to be pulling out a weapon when they were actually unarmed.

What is important to know about the police's perspective is that they too are acting out of the safety of their lives. When their lives are in danger or they are scared, their judgment is usually not reliable and they might not be in line with the expectations of a police officer.

American Police Vs. Others

You might be saying, "Well what about all of the other countries that suffer far less shootings by police officers?" It is a good question, but it is important to not underestimate the impact of the U.S. gun laws. Countries such as the UK and Wales prohibit gun ownership. In Iceland, where it is legal for citizens to carry guns, there are about 30 privately-owned guns per 100 people. Iceland is also one of the countries with extremely low rates of gun violence. Generally, most of the countries with low rates of police shootings do not give their citizens access to guns , thus, their police forces experience far less instances of being taken surprise by an armed suspect.

But can we really blame stressful situations for all of the police shootings? After all, there are a tremendous number of police shootings that were a result of a lack of training, according to several sources.

Police Training

While we do not want to disrespect our police officers and the difficult service jobs they have chosen to take up on our behalf, it is important to acknowledge the role of police training in police shootings. Police officers in the US are trained for an average of 19 weeks. That's a stark contrast to Norway, where police are trained for three years. In the United States, most police training is spent on how to protect themselves in dangerous situations.

The recent incident involving the arrest of Sandra Bland in Illinois demonstrated the ways in which police training could have been implemented better to prevent an unfortunate outcome i.e death. Bland died in a Texas jail cell. A video that showed the routine traffic stop resulted in her arrest. In the video, the officer asked Bland to exit the vehicle, which escalated the situation. Many critics claim that the officer did not take the steps to de-escalate the situation, and instead, only escalated it by asking Bland to step outside of the vehicle. The arrest eventually led to Bland's death, causing widespread controversy over police training.

The police are trained to include a wide variety of reasons as justification for shooting a suspect. For instance, a person reaching into their waistband or pockets. On average, police training includes about 60 hours for candidates to learn how to use their gun and only 8 hours to learn the use of force policy. 49 hours of police training are spent on defensive tactics and only 10 hours are spent on communication skills; 8 hours on de-escalation, crisis intervention and baton use.

In a nutshell, police training emphasizes the use of force rather than de-escalation, communication and understanding of different types of people.

According to the Texas Department of Public Safety, "The conventional wisdom has been that officers frequently have to make split-second decisions that have life-or-death consequences." The report adds, "While this is certainly the case in situations like active shooter incidents—when time is a critical factor—there are many other everyday situations where, after an initial assessment, it becomes clear that the more effective approach is to slow the situation down, maintain some distance between yourself and the subject to reduce the chance of a physical confrontation, and begin communicating with the person to seek a resolution."

Given the amount of police shootings involving minorities and mentally ill individuals, it is plausible to conclude these are both areas in which police could use more training. More than eight hours should be devoted to training on handling minority / police encounters to improve struggling relations between citizens and police forces around the country. The police should also incorporate lessons on how to handle mentally ill citizens into their training. Due to their state of mind, a mentally ill individual can be easily perceived as a threat by police officers. However, mentally ill individuals may have little control over their behavior and thus make irrational decisions during a police encounter. Individuals that suffer from mental illness may purposefully escalate a police encounter to be killed in a "suicide by police."

With full consideration of the nature of police training, we can improve our chances of not getting shot by the police. An understanding of the way the police are trained to handle a situation can help you understand how to not get shot by the police. Most importantly, we must consider the fact that police officers are trained to stay alive and protect the communities they serve. To do so, the police are trained to reduce the risk of danger as much as possible by making a fateful decision within a matter of seconds. Putting yourself in the officer's shoes may decrease your chances of getting shot and killed by the police. By demonstrating your willingness to be compliant and understanding of the officer's perspective during an encounter, you will be in a safer position.

Chapter 10. What To Do If You Are Licensed To Carry A Gun

If you are licensed to carry a gun, there are several things you should know about how to handle a police encounter to avoid getting shot. The shooting of Philando Castile, who was licensed to carry a gun, is an example of how much a gun can make a police encounter deadly.

Below is a list of concealed carry license laws for every U.S. state.

- **Shall Issue to Residents and Non-Residents:**

Alabama, Arizona, Arkansas, Florida, Georgia, Idaho, Illinois, Indiana, Iowa, Kansas, Maine, Minnesota, Mississippi, Missouri, Nevada, New Hampshire, North Carolina, North Dakota, Ohio, Oklahoma, Oregon, Pennsylvania, Puerto Rico, Rhode Island, South Carolina, Tennessee, Texas, Utah, Vermont, Virginia, and Washington.

- **May Issue to Residents Only:**

California, Delaware, New York City, Virgin Islands

- **May Issue to Residents and Non-Residents:**

Connecticut, District of Columbia, Hawaii, Maryland, Massachusetts, New Jersey, New York

- **Right Denied:**

American Samoa, N. Marian Islands.

Concealed carry license laws are important for everyone to know, because it can be the difference between a chaotic situation and an orderly one. If you are a gun owner, it is likely that you are already aware of your state's laws. If you are planning to purchase a weapon for self-defense, then you can avoid dangerous police encounters by having a thorough understanding of any state or local laws that may apply to gun holders. Lastly, if you plan to move or travel with your weapon, it is important to understand the laws of other states and how they may apply to you as a new resident or out of state visitor. The bottom line is to not assume one law applies to every situation. The police hold gun owners responsible for their actions and also expect gun owners to understand the limits of their concealed carry license. If you are caught in illegal possession of a weapon, it is likely that the officer will perceive you as a threat to their life as well as the public.

What To Do In A Traffic Stop

Being pulled over with a weapon in your car can go either way, but doesn't have to be a death sentence. If you have a license to carry a concealed weapon in your state, then you should also know what to do during a traffic stop. To the police, carrying a weapon is no joke and can rapidly escalate a typical traffic stop.

After getting pulled over, you will want to remain calm and keep your hands on the steering wheel (10 o'clock and 2 o'clock) after shutting off your engine. If you are on the passenger side, keep your hands in plain view or on the dashboard. It's probably not a good idea to start hiding your weapon or bringing it out into plain sight. The officer will take note of your movements before walking up to your window to speak with you. Any movements from a distance could make the officer perceive you as a potential threat.

The next, most important step of handling a traffic stop with a concealed weapon is to keep calm. If the officer asks do you have any weapons in the car, you can say something along the following lines, "Officer, I do have a concealed carry permit and currently have a firearm in my glove box." This last part is important because having one on you or out of a case, glove box or closed holster is illegal in most states and can lead to confusion or a misunderstanding.

After you have acknowledged your firearm, the next thing you should do is ask the police officer what they would like you to do. Giving the police officer control over the situation will reduce your chances of getting shot because it acknowledges your compliance and your willingness to be a responsible gun owner.

Before you retrieve your driver's license and other motorist documents, make sure to inform the police officer of your firearm location. If you want to be completely safe, you can let the officer know you will feel more comfortable if he / she retrieved your license or firearm. Upon showing the officer your driver's license, it is a good idea to show them your concealed weapons permit as well. Make sure to move extremely slow and show no signs of suspicious behavior.

In a situation such as this, putting yourself in the officer's shoes can save your life. The police have no idea what kind of person you are or your criminal history or lack of. From their perspective, safety is the number one priority and they will not be likely to take many risks to put their lives in danger.

When you have a license to carry a firearm, you should also be looking into the local and state laws that may apply to you. For example, some states require you to inform the police upfront that you are carrying a firearm. If you are not in one of those states, keep your mouth shut unless they ask you about weapons. Thus, you should be aware of any laws that apply to you in your area.

Conclusion

In this book, we have discussed how to not get shot by the police. Such a discussion began with a perhaps, overdramatic solution, which is to move to another country. Several European nations have far lower instances of police shootings than America and, thus, if you really want to reduce your chances of being shot by the police, you should investigate some of these possibilities more thoroughly. We also discussed the role that race plays in police shootings. Although it was revealed that more white people are shot by police than any other ethnicity in 2015, African American people were disproportionately represented. Specifically, police shootings of unarmed, African American males were shown to be an area of concern and a source of controversy in on-going debates over race, gun regulations, and police brutality.

Although the evidence of police bias against African American males is problematic, it should also be noted that anyone could be shot by the police. Home encounters, traffic stops, and walk stops are all situations in which a police encounter can quickly escalate into something much more serious. If you have no reason to fear a police stop, then there will be less of a chance for the police to suspect you of committing a crime for which you were not the responsible party.

In general, you can count on several tactics to help you get through any of the three police stops. These include staying calm, being patient and polite with the police, and letting them do most of the talking.

However, you should understand that no one or set of rules can totally exclude you from being shot by the police. As we have seen in the past several months, police shootings of unarmed individuals are becoming increasingly common in America. Due to the current conditions of our social and political landscape, it is paramount to avoid falling into the assumption that "law abiding" citizens are immune to police shootings. This traditional black-and-white lifestyle fails to account for the gray areas in which hundreds of legal battles and protests have erupted across the country.

Showing compliance and demonstrating your rights as a citizen or non-citizen is a thin line to walk. Balancing both aspects of a police encounter takes practice and time to digest the information regarding each type of police stop, which includes consensual encounters, investigative detention, and arrests. While it is important to practice your rights, it is far more important to stay alive.

As a citizen, your survival depends on the police's decision making, which often depends on your behavior. If you choose to exercise your rights under the 4th amendment, for example, then you should be extra careful with the way you communicate this information to the police. It is your job to prevent the situation from progressing into an argument, which may only cause the officer to look for reasons to believe you are guilty of committing a crime. The next thing you know is the police can and will use excessive force if they believe you to be a dangerous threat to their lives. This scenario is just an example of how quickly a police stop can escalate and greatly increase your chances of being shot. Thus, while practicing your rights is worthwhile, it is also worthwhile to do so safely and calmly so you will not get shot by cops.

THE DAY I DIED

As I lay here, while my family is grieving by my coffin,

Another victim of a problem that occurs way too often.

It's a problem that occurs frequently, but mostly to African American Males.

It's the problem of our family and friends being shot by cops without even taking them to jail.

I had just gotten out of my bed to begin a brand new day,

To put in eight hours or more, in order to earn a full day's pay.

So I got into my car, to drive off to my job,

Enjoying the music on the radio, as I puffed on my "Black and Mild Cigar".

I was chilling and jamming and just enjoying the early morning breeze,

Until I looked into my mirror and saw-flashing red lights that appeared with ease.

I pulled my car over and took out my license and registration to keep it near

Knowing that this situation can bring problems of despair.

The cop came over to my window to check out my I.D. I cooperated fully,

Than I asked him "What could the problem possibly be?"

He told me my taillight was out, but advised me not to get out of the car

Then preceded to check my tag, the car's exterior and then he pulled the back door ajar.

I began to view the inside of the car, making sure everything was okay,

Then I spotted a half of joint, that my friend had left the previous day.

Fear over shadowed me, as I didn't know what to do,

So I threw it out of the window, to get it out of view.

He then asked me, what I threw out of the window. Just then fear upon me came,

I told him, "Nothing officer." He then said, "I know, real well that game."

He walked up to the joint and picked it up off the ground,

Then said; "You are under arrest for pot possession, and I'm taking you down.

I pleaded, "I don't do drugs, give me a drug or lie detector test, that joint's not even mine.

You see, today is payday; I've got bills to pay and I must get to work on time".

I asked again, "Please can you give me a ticket or something because I can't miss work today" ?

He said: "You are going to jail, come on Boy, you just can't have your way.

He said: "you committed a crime and today no work you'll see.

At this point I said to myself, "I'll chance it, and will make a run and flee.

As I fled, I began to hear the sound of gun shots: Pow, pow, pow ,

Another person shot in the back, another American down.

Just then I woke up in a cold sweat, and realized it was all a dream.

Suddenly a burden was lifted off my shoulders, and I was grateful to have been redeemed.

I reflected on the situation and how it could have turned out the other way,

and I am thankful it didn't happen like that, so I could see another day.

Just then I thought of my brothers and sisters, throughout the various towns,

For whatever color they might be, and I thought, "A change is needed now".

Whatever happened to "Officer Friendly"? , He knew the community and the community knew him as well.

He would've known that I had no priors, and never even been to jail. .

Have you ever wondered how a person who did mass killings at a movie or a church,

Was easily taken to jail, without even getting hurt?

But for a traffic stop, possession or for selling cigarettes in front of a store, resulted in instant departures of men from this earth forever more.

A solution to this problem is needed right away.

We must end these police shootings and killings come what may.

We need to change our priorities like, "Shooting to Halt" in the arm or legs,

Rather than, Shooting to Kill", in the head or back that results in an early grave.

There is an urgent need for sensitivity training and open dialogue,

New De-escalation techniques by police and mutual respect to all

By: Jeanette Strachan

Learn more at:

www.HowNotToGetShotByCops.com

www.Facebook.com/NotShotByCops

Instagram: @NotShotByCops

Twitter: @NotShotByCops

Make sure to watch the videos on our YouTube channel.

FOOTNOTES AND SOURCES CITED

1. https://www.washingtonpost.com/graphics/national/police-shootings/

2. http://www.theguardian.com/us-news/ng-interactive/2015/jun/01/the-counted-police-killings-us-database

3. http://blacklivesmatter.com/

4. http://www.nytimes.com/2016/07/22/us/groups-unite-across-america-to-protest-police-shootings.html?_r=0

5. https://www.sptdc.com/

6. http://www.freedom-now.org/

7. http://www.miamiherald.com/news/local/crime/article94009242.html

8. http://www.nytimes.com/2016/07/09/us/dallas-police-shooting.html

9. http://thedailybanter.com/2014/08/uk-police-stop-someone-knife/

10. http://thedailybanter.com/2014/08/uk-police-stop-someone-knife/

11. https://www.theguardian.com/us-news/2015/jun/09/the-counted-police-killings-us-vs-other-countries

12. http://www.huffingtonpost.com/entry/reduce-chances-shot-by-police_us_577d2192e4b09b4c43c1c53a

13. http://www.nytimes.com/2015/12/27/us/chicago-police-fatally-shoot-2-raising-new-questions-for-a-force-under-scrutiny.html?_r=1

14. https://www.washingtonpost.com/posttv/editorial/what_to_do_when_you_feel_overwhelmed-by-more-police-shootings/2015/07/31/b42ff754-3793-11e5-ab7b-6416d97c73c2_video.html

15. http://www.businessinsider.com/david-eckerts-traffic-stop-in-new-mexico-2013-11

16.
http://www.slate.com/blogs/crime/2012/11/30/stop_and_frisk_florida_is_there_such_thing_as_a_consensual_police_encounter.html

17. http://www.nytimes.com/2015/06/10/us/los-angeles-police-officers-acted-improperly-in-shooting-of-ezell-ford-commission-finds.html?_r=0

18. http://www.nytimes.com/2016/07/29/nyregion/is-a-police-shooting-a-crime-it-depends-on-the-officers-point-of-view.html?_r=0

19. http://www.today.com/news/shoot-or-not-shoot-researchers-test-how-police-react-danger-t4961

20. http://qz.com/727941/how-do-police-handle-violence-in-countries-where-officers-dont-carry-guns/

21. http://fusion.net/story/186239/police-training-guns-chart/

22. https://www.washingtonpost.com/posttv/national/video-shows-fatal-shooting-of-tulsa-man-by-reserve-deputy/2015/04/12/72de187a-e13b-11e4-ae0f-f8c46aa8c3a4_video.html

23. https://www.washingtonpost.com/posttv/national/video-shows-fatal-shooting-of-tulsa-man-by-reserve-deputy/2015/04/12/72de187a-e13b-11e4-ae0f-f8c46aa8c3a4_video.html

24. http://www.myajc.com/news/news/crime-law/gbi-officers-respond-to-wrong-house-shoot-homeowne/nrcj8/

25. https://en.wikipedia.org/wiki/Shooting_of_Trayvon_Martin

26. http://articles.sun-sentinel.com/1987-03-01/news/8701130481_1_metro-dade-detectives-crack-cocaine

27.   http://www.miaminewtimes.com/news/miami-gardens-has-gone-from-middle-class-dream-for-black-residents-to-total-embarrassment-7530812

28. http://fusion.net/story/5568/florida-citys-stop-frisk-nabs-thousands-of-kids-finds-5-year-olds-suspicious/

29. https://en.wikipedia.org/wiki/Kathryn_Johnston_shooting